ME!

By Deidré Sample

Illustrated by Cameron Wilson

WHEN YOU LOOK AT ME...

WHAT DO YOU SEE?

DO YOU SEE A WINNER? A CHAMPION? A STAR?

DO YOU SEE A STRONG,

BRAVE...

AND WONDERFUL ME?

DO YOU SEE SOMEONE WHO IS DESTINED FOR GREATNESS?

NO MATTER WHAT ANYONE ELSE SEES, WHAT MATTERS MOST IS WHAT I BELIEVE ABOUT ME.

What I believe about ME determines my victory.

Mirror, mirror on the wall
LOOK AT ME
standing brave and tall.

LOOK AT ME
beating all the odds.

destined for greater and greater heights

I am magnificently created
and I know that from within.

My worth comes from the inside
It's my power to win and I cannot hide.